Face Everything And Rise

Discover Your Awesome

Barry Collins

Face Everything And Roar

Discover Your Awesome

Barry Collins

ISBN 978-1539552543

1st Edition 2016

For my teachers

Many people have provided valuable lessons to me in life, and so this is for them. Thank you Tolly Burkan for teaching the world to firewalk.

To my fire brothers, Tim Spencer, Jon Boys & Steve Consalvez, who have my love and trust always, thank you for walking beside me on my journey, and teach me the value of true friends.

To my children & grandchildren for teaching me to stay young. My brother & sister for teaching me that life is for living, because we can't know the future.

To my mother, father & step-father for being the people they were as I grew up, so that I could learn to be the man I have become.

And to my wife, Marina, for teaching me that true love can conquer all and make dreams come true. I love you eternally.

Introduction

This book is not for you if you already feel completely fulfilled, and your life truly satisfies you in every way. If, however, you have a sense that spending the foreseeable future doing the same as yesterday, today and tomorrow, just isn't going cut it, then this just might be the sign you've been waiting for...

Getting Started

Congratulations! Creating change in your life requires action. Even just the smallest step will be a step in the right direction if done intentionally, and that's exactly what you have done by starting this book. Keep going, let the momentum build, and get ready to roar... Your future is waiting!

1 History

If The World Is Cold, Make It Your Business To Build Fires.

In The Beginning...

Fire worship, as a rite of purification, healing, initiation and passage, has shown up time and time again across the globe. Different tribes and cultures across time have recognised and embraced the positive effect that fire and firewalking has for warming and nourishing the human spirit. Firewalking has been recognised by popular culture as a powerful tool for change, empowerment & self development.

The exact origins of firewalking are lost in the mists of time, but we do know that Africa, considered the birthplace of humankind, has a long history of firewalking and fire dancing. The earliest known reference to firewalking dates to 1200 BC. The oldest recorded firewalk was over 4000 years ago in India, when two Brahmin priests were competing to see who could walk further, and this feat was written down in the historical records of that time.

Romans were exempted from paying taxes if they could demonstrate their ability to walk on fire without burning. !Kung Bushmen in Africa used fire dance as a powerful healing ritual for their tribe. Their ceremony not only included firewalking, but also rolling on the fire. In Bali, fire dancing is the coming of age ritual for seven-year-old girls. The Greek Anastenarides danced on hot coals for hours to honour Saint Constantine and Saint Helen. The Kahunas of Hawaii let molten lava harden just enough to hold their weight before walking on it.

In Bali, the mystical South Sea island, it is not the men who dance on the fire, but young girls. In India, Tibet, Sri Lanka, China, Japan and Argentina, to mention a few, people dance and walk, joyously, solemnly, exuberantly, or devotionally across fire. In the Hindu fire ceremony Agni Hotra, fire is used to purify the physical and spiritual atmosphere and in Peru the flame is used to spiritually uplift participants in the fire-ceremony.

There are even references to firewalking in the Bible:

> Can one go upon hot coals, and his feet not be burned? (From Proverbs 6:28)

> When thou walkest through the fire, thou shalt not be burned (From Isaiah 43:2).

So what do all these ancient people and cultures know that we don't? They have turned their reverence of fire into ceremonies and rituals to enhance their well-being and communities, understanding that the benefits of firewalking clearly outweigh the risks.

Firewalking In Modern Times

In 1977, 29 year old Tolly Burkan was introduced to firewalking for the first time, and was so transformed by the experience, he immediately wanted to share it with as many people as possible. He struggled to understand why more people weren't teaching firewalking, and for 7 years he was the only person on the planet teaching firewalking!

He researched the subject in great depth and found that for every theory explaining why firewalkers could safely cross the embers, there was another theory that directly contradicted it.

In 1978, already having been involved in the human-potential movement since 1973, he began offering firewalking as part of a personal development seminar. Until 1982, he continued to teach firewalking on a limited scale, but at this time contacted the media and what would become known as the Global Firewalking Movement was born...

In 1983, Tolly taught Tony Robbins how to firewalk. Not only did Tony immediately decide that he himself also wanted to teach firewalking classes, he proved to be a master at generating additional publicity. By early 1984, Tony's firewalking classes were drawing hundreds of people. He also targeted the celebrity market, and suddenly, many notables from Hollywood were walking on fire. This, of course, fuelled even more media attention.

Tony started doing firewalks for U.S. corporations. However, as companies learned that he was using the "Fear into Power" format developed by Tolly Burkan, many sought him out directly. Over time the list of corporations grew to include companies such as Microsoft, American Express, RE/MAX International and Coca-Cola.

In the 80's, Tolly established the Firewalking Institute of Research & Education (F.I.R.E.) to certify Firewalk Instructors, but many thought they could conduct firewalks without having attended the training, and, not surprisingly, the results were disastrous. If you choose to have the experience of firewalking, ensure your event is led by a certified instructor.

Over the years the movement continued to grow, but then there was a paradigm shift when US President Bill Clinton crossed the coals in 1993, and since then numerous top level CEO's and celebrities have fire walked, not least of which was Oprah Winfrey in 2011 with Tony Robbins. All of this only served to grow the global firewalking movement.

In recent years, Tolly parted company with F.I.R.E. and, with the help of Steve Consalvez & Kevin Axtell, created The Firewalking Centre, and no longer taught his now famous "Fear Into Power" seminar, but focused on teaching instructors to carry his message and teachings to humanity.

In 2016 Tolly announced his intention to teach his last ever Firewalking Mastery program to just 8 people before retiring at midnight on 31st December, 2016.

I was one of those 8 people, and this is my story...

Barry Collins

2

Taking The First Step...

Time is the fire in which we all burn

Accidents Happen

My life began to change by accident. It wasn't planned, it just happened. Like so many of the great things in life, the things that are the most rewarding, I had absolutely no intention whatsoever of things turning out the way they did.

If you are married, or in a relationship, you most likely didn't go out having made the decision to meet your soul mate that day... it just happened! Some people say that the universe will support and guide you if you are following your destiny - I think there may be something in that!

We all have our own personal bucket lists, whether we talk about them or not. To run with the bulls in Pamplona, to see the world from the top of Kilimanjaro, learn to prepare sushi, read War and Peace, you'll know what's on yours (and the things on it you've already achieved) and I knew one of the things on mine was a firewalk.

I hadn't been actively looking to do one, I was just aware that one day, at some point, I wanted to be able to say I had done a firewalk, but like so many things in life that we want, I wasn't doing anything to 'make' it happen. I was just happy knowing that there was something to look forward to, at some point in the future. Then my wife, Marina, suggested we help a friend who was in the middle of a long term fundraising campaign for charity, but was still working towards hitting her target amount. The plan was to organise a firewalk event, with delegates raising sponsorship to contribute to our friends campaign.

Working in the personal development field for a number of years, and having made many contacts, we asked for recommendations for someone that would provide such an event at a location near us, and the same name kept coming up...

Spark Of Madness

After many conversations with the people that we had engaged to provide the event, we had a date, a venue and a cause. Now, all we needed was to get our friends on board and get them involved - easier said than done!

Most of the conversations went something like this:

Me: How do you fancy joining me on a firewalk?

Them: What's a firewalk?

Me: The clue is in the name, but essentially walking bare foot over a bed of glowing coals.

What followed was them either staring at me dumbfounded, running away, or asking any number of questions that were all placing a question mark over my sanity, however, enough people 'got it' and agreed to take part, that allowed us to proceed and meet the minimum number requirements.

The next two months were spent explaining to people that I had had a recent psych evaluation, and got the all clear, which meant that, yes, I knew what I was asking them to sponsor me for, and I was okay with it.

What surprised me was the generosity of the people I sought sponsorship from. I think when I first approached them to take part, and explained that if they weren't taking part they could still support the cause by sponsoring me, they saw an opportunity for their generosity to get them off the hook. Consequently, the money we raised far exceed our expectations, but I'll come to that...

Exercise 1

1. Think of something you have done, even though it scared you to do it.
2. Remember in detail what it was like after you had done it. Remember what you saw, what you heard and how you felt.
3. Take a moment to fully reconnect with the experience.
4. Recall all the reasons that motivated you to do it, in spite of the fear.
5. Identify all the positive consequences as a result of having achieved it.

Notes

3

Spark To A Flame

Find what sparks a light in you, so that in your own way, you may illuminate the world

Arrival

Three months after we first had made the initial enquiries, the day of our firewalk arrived, and I'll be frank, I was excited and terrified in equal amounts. We arrived an hour before other delegates to meet the instructor and crew, and to make sure everything was running to plan.

After that we were simply a delegate attending the event, with no idea of what lay ahead other than at some point we would be walking on red hot coals. Other delegates, our friends, all arrived sharing in the uncertainty and trepidation we were all feeling by that point. And then we started...

Say Goodbye To Your Comfort Zone

Over the next hour or so, as a group we were gently and gradually coerced out of our respective comfort zones through a number of 'thought exercises', designed to guide us towards *the* right state, as opposed to *a* right state. The right state is the optimal state of being fully present, and connected with all the positive resources we all have within us, all of the time, but through the life we have led, we have forgotten how to access.

I honestly thought the preparation part was going to be very 'left-brain', technical in its content explaining how to walk safely on fire. I could not have been any further from the truth. The exercises asked us to talk openly about our fears, and for many, it was with someone they had only met that evening, but that is the point, to do something you wouldn't normally do, and so the evening proceeded, and as it did I began to see that this was not about walking on fire at all. I'm not going to lie to you, doing some of the exercises did make me, and others, feel a little uncomfortable, but that was the point. Doing something you've never done before, or that you wouldn't normally choose to do is where the opportunity to grow is, to expand your experience and become more than you thought you were, because you can begin to observe how the way you think creates your experience.

Everything we did that evening was a metaphor for the way so many of us choose to live our lives. We don't attempt things because we focus on the 'what-if's'. We buy in to the stories we tell ourselves in an attempt to keep ourselves safe, but we sacrifice opportunities for joy and fulfilment for comfort and familiarity.

The exercises led us to discover what we believed and how those beliefs influenced the behaviours we adopted, that were in fact holding us back, and then provided the opportunity to exorcise our limiting beliefs and begin the process of adjusting to a world with no limits, other than those we place on ourselves.

The time flew by as we delved deeper and deeper in to the mindset of success and achievement, and explored the relationship we have with our own unconscious, and how to make it work *for* us, instead of against us. Before we knew it, the time had come to light the fire.

We made our way from the relative comfort of the room we had been in, out in to the dwindling daylight, to the nearby area where the tenders and been hard at work, building the fire and preparing for the evenings main event.

As a group we now grasped this was about so much more than just walking on fire. It was something different for each of us and we were asked to consider what it would mean later when we crossed the coals. And then the fire was lit. The height of the flames and the intensity of the heat took me by surprise, and I think it was about this time I thought to myself, "this sh*t just got real!"

After lighting the fire, we returned indoors and we spent a little time *really* pushing the limits of what we believed we were capable of, in ways that I could not have guessed, but now understand were just stepping stones on the path to being ready to walk on fire...

Crossing To The Other Side

The time finally arrived, and we were led outside, most of us bubbling over with nervous excitement. The rhythmic beats of the music we had been repeatedly listening to for the last few hours, playing in our minds, maintaining the state we had built within ourselves and each other. And then we saw it... the most beautiful, mesmerising and intimidating thing I have ever seen in my life.

Twelve feet of glowing embers, spread out, inviting us, calling to us. As the crew tended to the walk, we were instructed to remove our socks & shoes, an 'get ready'. I remember I had never been as acutely aware of the sensation of the ground beneath my feet as I was at that moment. I could feel the subtle differences in the surface I was standing on as the cold of the ground began to have an effect on my feet.

And then they were off! So caught up in my own thinking I was unaware that the walk had been announced open, and people were already crossing. Torn between becoming absorbed in what was happening before me, and quickly going through the list of tools we'd been armed with to get ourselves 'in the zone', I realised I had to focus. Not consciously realising I was doing it, I stepped forward, and, just like we had been shown, I began to walk...

Breaking Free

Before I was really aware it was happening, I was on the other side, and as I struggled to comprehend exactly what I'd just done, I became aware of the cheering and clapping, from participants and supporters alike. Then it happened - the world seemed to irreversibly tilt on its axis!

The surge of adrenaline induced a euphoric like state as we celebrated as a group as people continued to cross the coals. Hugs were exchanged, cheers were shared, and then I was back at the start, my hand held by the friend we were helping to raise money, and together we crossed a second time. Cameras flashed, cheers went up, we hugged, we clapped, and the world continued to shift...

Breaking Through

Afterwards during the debrief, we were told that as a group, the 23 people in the room had raised in excess of £4,000 for charity in just one night. Our friend had smashed through her fundraising target, and was now on her way to doubling it. We took the valuable lessons we had learned, and headed for home.

Exercise 2

1. Identify something you've been putting off.
2. Consider the reason(s) you have not started.
3. For every reason you have not started, write down two benefits you'll gain after completing it.
4. Imagine feeling the same way as in the previous exercise, after completing *this* adventure. Immerse yourself in the experience. Notice what you see, what you hear and what you feel.
5. As you are absorbed in the experience, identify what would be the smallest step you could take towards completing the task, and do it.

Notes

4

Forest Fire

What you wish to ignite in others, must first burn within yourself

Stirring The Embers

If you've ever done something that *really* pushed you beyond your comfort zone, you'll already understand the sense of achievement that I woke up with the next day. The natural high from physiological changes as a result of the previous evening, could not be denied. I bounced out of bed and embraced the day ahead. This was not what I would class as normal behaviour at that time...

Having left my 25 year corporate career behind two years earlier, I had been doing something I love, I was accustomed to waking up and looking forward to the day ahead, but this was most definitely different, this was so much more.

Over the next couple of weeks, on several occasions I spoke to the instructor who had guided us safely across the coals, each time finding out a little more about the firewalking community, and beginning to see how it could fit with the work I already did with hypnotherapy, coaching & NLP (Neuro-Linguistic Programming) assisting others become the best version of themselves. These discussions eventually led me to speak to Steve Consalvez, the UK's only Master Certifying Firewalking Instructor. It was like getting a glimpse of the wizard when the wind catches the curtain for just a moment, and I knew at that moment, at least at some level, that there was fire in my soul.

Fanning The Flame

Six short weeks later, I arrived at the UK's only dedicated Firewalk Instructor Training (F.I.T.) centre in Cambridgeshire. During the time I spent there, I made friends that will be friends for life, and I know that if I ever really needed them, they would be there, and I for them if they called. It's the same bond that survivors of tragedies share. When you have been through something so intense, so transformative, that only those who have experienced it, can fully comprehend the monumental affect it has on the rest of your life, the connection you share with those people is profound and unshakeable.

I won't share the contents of the training here, as one reason you may be reading this is as a precursor to attending the F.I.T, and an important part of the process is facing the exercises you are invited to participate in during the training without any preparation - trust me when I tell you, it's probably better that way!

What I will tell you is you will learn to acknowledge the small voice within that guides people to what is 'safe', what is 'familiar' & what is 'comfortable'. That voice can be *very* persuasive, however once you realise how much the beliefs you've been holding on to, have in fact held you back from achieving your dreams, you just might choose to let them go.

Whether it's success in business, in love, with money, or any other area of your life, the beliefs you are invested in ultimately determine the level of success you achieve. How can you hope to empower others, to help them connect with their own personal power, if you still hold on to the part of you that stops you chasing down your dreams relentlessly, and make them a reality?

> Two monks were returning from market, when they came upon a young maiden crying on the banks of a river, unable to cross.
>
> She addressed the elder monk, "Please can you help me cross the river?" He immediately replied, "Of course. Climb upon my back, I shall carry you across the river"
>
> The novice monk was dismayed. As he considered the vows of chastity & silence that both monks had taken upon entering the monastery, he struggled to come to terms with what he had just witnessed.
>
> The elder monk returned from the other side of the river and they continued on their way. After a couple of miles the novice monk could contain himself no longer, and had to ask "Brother, we took a vow of silence, forbidding us to speak outside the monastery, and a vow of chastity, forbidding us to even make eye contact with a woman, let alone physical contact! How could you so easily forget these vows?"
>
> The elder monk stopped and turned to the young monk and said, "The woman needed help and I put her down on the other side of the river. Why do you carry her still?"

Feeding The Fire

In the weeks that followed my certification as an instructor, I did a number of events, and a strange thing happened when I stepped on stage - an unexpected, yet welcome, calmness came over me. I knew that I had been trained by one of the best in the world, and had the hands on experience that had allowed me to apply that knowledge away from the training room, and know that whatever happened, I had been prepared and equipped to deal with anything.

With each event, my confidence in my knowledge and ability continued to grow, but this wasn't limited just to my events. I found that other parts of my life had also evolved, and the curveballs that life sometimes throws were less of a negative experience, but rather an opportunity to expand my experiences, and in doing so learn that there was little that could knock me down or at least not keep me down for long, if I chose not to let it!

I'm not going to pretend it was all plain sailing along the way, but problems seemed less 'problematic', and opportunities seemed to present themselves more often. Through all of this I was in regular contact with Steve and his team who had trained me, and who continued to offer advice and guidance when I sought it.

I made an initial enquiry about returning to assist in future trainings, and it was agreed that there would benefits for both of us.

Wildfire

In between my own events, I returned to Firewalking UK's headquarters to assist in welcoming more instructors to the global firewalking movement, including Marina, who had also caught the fire-bug. Together we present our own events, continuing to raise thousands of pounds for local charities & deserving causes, and changing countless lives along the way. Although many of our events were only a few hours, the process we take participants through, the way we ask them to think, is creating in others the kind of change we had both experienced attending the F.I.T.

Looking back I can't believe I waited so long to follow my dream, but at the same time I can understand why I did. I worked in an environment that expected conformity, in the way that any large organisation does - they have processes to follow to maintain order, they have systems to ensure consistency, and after 25 years in that mindset, it's no wonder I didn't realise what I was actually capable of. I had learned to follow, to fit in, to *conform!*

> There was a lion who had grown up in a flock of sheep, and so had no consciousness that he was a lion. He didn't know he was a lion. He'd eat grass like a sheep, he'd bleat like a sheep.
>
> One day a mighty lion leaped out of the jungle, in to the middle of the pack, and gave a mighty roar. The sheep scattered, bleating as they did. The mighty lion was surprised to see a lion running away with the pack, and so he gave chase and caught him.
>
> The lion begged, "Please don't eat me! Please don't eat me!"
>
> The mighty lion grabbed him by the mane, and dragged him to the lake, "Look!"
>
> And for the first time, the lion who thought he was a sheep saw his reflection. He looked at the mighty lion. He looked at his reflection, and let out a mighty roar.

> The mighty lion said, "This is who you truly are. Even before I showed you, this is who you were, because this is what you truly are"

It would have been so easy for me to continue along the path I had been on. It was safe & secure, but it hadn't really fulfilled me... it wasn't who I was.

Seeing people arrive at our events, full of uncertainty and a trepidation, fills me with excitement at the prospect of, if I pay attention and get my message across, seeing them all leave with renewed belief in themselves, full of hope and confidence about the future. They may not have all the answers when they leave, but you will have a much better chance of finding them when you believe the answers are out there.

Exercise 3

1. If you knew you couldn't fail, what would choose to do?
2. Now imagine yourself having achieved it. Notice what you see, what you hear and how you feel.
3. Start to work backwards from that achievement to where you are now, identifying each preceding step until you have a step-by-step strategy to get there.
4. Decide when you are going to take the first step towards achieving your dream

Notes

5

Inferno

Those who walk through fire leave sparks of light everywhere they go

Lessons & Blessings

The journey of discovery you are on will hold many blessings for you, and these are always welcome, but not always immediately apparent. My journey has held many lessons for me, which have allowed me to continue on my chosen path. Your path will be littered with hidden lessons. You may not always be able to identify the lesson straight away, but with a little perseverance, it will be revealed when you are ready to receive it.

When you accept the lesson with humility, and a willingness to learn, you discover the blessing within. Some of the hardest things we face in life, can be the most rewarding, and prepare us to achieve a future of our own creation, not one designed by others. Some will require determination and effort, others will require focus and an open mind.

> Once there was a Chinese farmer who worked his poor farm together with his son and their horse. When the horse ran off one day, neighbours came to say, "How unfortunate for you!" The farmer replied, "Maybe..."
>
> When the horse returned, followed by a herd of wild horses, the neighbours gathered around and exclaimed, "What good luck for you!" The farmer stayed calm and replied, "Maybe..."

> While trying to tame one of the new wild horses, the farmer's son fell, and broke his leg. He had to rest up and couldn't help with the farm chores. "How sad for you", the neighbours cried, "Maybe..." said the farmer.
>
> Shortly thereafter, a neighbouring army threatened the farmer's village. All the young men in the village were drafted to fight the invaders. Many died. But the farmer's son had been left out of the fighting because of his broken leg. People said to the farmer, "What a good thing your son couldn't fight!" All the farmer said was, "Maybe..."

Some people tell me how lucky I am to be able to do something I love doing, and be able to call it work. And yet the years I spent looking for the way to leave an unfulfilling career, and find something more rewarding didn't feel lucky - They felt like hard work. It took commitment to continue looking for the way out, when it seemed that there wasn't one. I don't think luck was the biggest factor. The belief that I could find the way out, created far more opportunities and possibilities than luck ever did.

Thoughts Are Things

When you look for what could go wrong, you will find that, in life, there are an infinite number of outcomes, most of them negative and unwanted. However, when you pay attention to, and focus on what could go right, it will begin to happen far more of the time.

After you cross a bed of glowing embers for the first time, something almost magical happens... a new world of possibilities opens up for you.

Some people will *choose* to return to work the next day, and fall back in to their old routines, of thinking, as well as doing, *but that is a choice!*

You can also choose to hold on to that sense of wonder that fills you when you realise the world was *not* holding you back, *you* were holding *you* back, but not any more. I've spoken to people who, after firewalking, have had minor surgery without anaesthetic, because they are acutely aware of how their thoughts create their experience. Others who have decided to follow their dreams, and successfully apply for positions they previously thought beyond them.

Your enthusiasm for life can be rekindled when you realise there's more out there than just putting your head down, and getting on with doing the same thing for the rest of your life if you don't enjoy it. Take the immense joy, excitement and belief that you are truly awesome that fills you after walking on fire, and take that out in to the world and share it!

Exercise 4

1. Think about all of the great achievements in your life, and write down as many as you can think of that make you feel proud when you think about them.
2. Think about all the people who have helped you become the person you are. Realise that even those people who have wronged you in some way, are in part responsible for you becoming the awesome individual you are today. Make a list of all the people you would thank - *all* of them.
3. From that list choose one person that you perhaps don't tell often enough how important they are, and how grateful you are to have them in your life, that you love them. Call them, and tell them - BUT... don't tell them anything about this book. Just tell them you were thinking about them and wanted to let them know how grateful you are you know them.

Notes

6

Afterglow

Your spark can become a flame and change everything

Rise From The Flames

You have probably already figured it out by now, but just in case let me be clear on one thing... Firewalking has very little to do with walking on fire!

It's not the most useful skill to have. You'll never swing that job interview based on your ability to stride confidently across 12 feet of glowing embers. Your bank manager is not more likely to approve your loan application as a result of your ability to trust your body to safely carry beyond the glowing coals in front of you... or at least not directly.

Whilst firewalking promises none of these things, what it does offer is the chance for you discover the most awesome, the mot powerful, the most confident you that there is. And so when you're in that interview, or pitching your business plan to your bank manager, all the very best qualities you have will shine through.

If you allow it to, the fire will show you what is already within you. We all have remarkable capabilities within us, to be kind, to be strong, to love, to support, to help, to allow the light that resides within each of to truly shine brightly. Life will sometimes challenge you, but as you make your way through life, you will continue to grow, and each challenge you overcome will reward you with a glimpse of your potential.

We can never know what is impossible, we can only ever know what is possible. Impossible is just the label we put on things we haven't figured out yet. Before 1903 and the Wright brothers, people didn't believe that man could fly. In 1961, Yuri Gagarin was the first man in space. Until then people didn't believe it was possible. Life is full of mysteries and puzzles. You just might be the first to solve one of them.

When we think of all the men and women who have changed the world, the ones we remember are the ones who did something, not just for themselves, but for humanity at large. Alexander Fleming, Florence Nightingale, Albert Einstein, Nelson Mandela, Mahatma Gandhi, they all became more, not by doing something for themselves, but by doing something for others.

When we follow a path that allows us to serve others, we find in ourselves something that can sometimes remain hidden when we endeavour in selfish pursuits. Some may say it's our desire not to let others down, but I like to think that at some deep unconscious level, we understand that to tap in to that unlimited potential, we have to engage in selfless acts of kindness.

It may start with being kind to yourself, as the benefit to others is a 'you' that can see the best in people, including yourself, but when you extend that kindness to others, without expectation of reciprocation or reward, there's a kind of magic that happens. The person you do a kindness for, will be more likely to do a kindness for others, and you can probably guess where that leads...

Exercise 5

1. Take a moment to remember the last time that someone did something kind for you, without seeking reward or thanks. Remember how it made you feel.
2. Make a conscious choice to do something kind for someone today. It doesn't need to be something big, it doesn't need to be for someone you know. Now do it without recognition, or the need for thanks.
3. Notice how good you feel as a result of someone providing you the opportunity to serve them, selflessly.

Notes

7

Conclusion

The most powerful force on earth is the human soul on fire.

It all starts with one step - you making a choice, a decision. If you choose to firewalk, I can honestly say it will be one of the most rewarding experiences in your life, but be prepared for your world to change, because it will - If you let it.

When you make deliberate choices and decisions in life, you are creating your own future, you are designing your own destiny.

So many people stumble through life unaware of the moments of choice they are missing. You look around and see others stumbling along and mistakenly believe that you are just like all those people that surround you, destined for mediocrity and banality.

Let me grab you by the mane, and drag you to the lake, and show you your reflection...

"This is who you truly are. Even before I showed you, this is who you were, because this is what you truly are. You are able to face everything and roar"